5 LESSONS FROM POPE FRANCIS

Oswald Sobrino, Ph.D.

Sobrino Works

CONTENTS

Title Page

Copyright

Abbreviations and References

Introduction

Chapter 1 The "Throwaway World"   1

Chapter 2 Embracing the Stranger   5

Chapter 3 Beyond Borders   11

Chapter 4 The Politics of Social Friendship   14

Chapter 5 Dialogue as Social Friendship   18

Epilogue: The Role of Religion   24

About The Author   27

ABBREVIATIONS AND REFERENCES

5 Lessons from John Dewey: Oswald Sobrino, *5 Lessons from John Dewey* (Sobrino Works, 2023).

Cambridge Dictionary: Available at:

https://dictionary.cambridge.org/

FT: *Fratelli Tutti* ("All Brethren"). Encyclical Letter of Pope Francis on Fraternity and Social Friendship, dated October 3, 2020, in the eighth year of his pontificate. Available at:

https://www.vatican.va/content/francesco/en/encyclicals/documents/papa-francesco_20201003_enciclica-fratelli-tutti.html

Id.: having the same citation as the immediately previous citation; from *idem* ("same" in Latin).

Lohnes: Lohnes, K. and Lowne, Cathy. "The Stranger." *Encyclopedia Britannica*, May 5, 2020. Available at:

https://www.britannica.com/topic/The-Stranger-novel-by-Camus

NRSV Updated Edition: New Revised Standard Version, Updated Edition. Copyright © 2021 National Council of Churches of Christ in the United States of America. Used by permission. All rights reserved worldwide. Available at https://www.biblegateway.com/.

Patterson: Orlando Patterson, *Slavery and Social Death: A*

Comparative Study (Harvard University Press, 2018; with a new preface).

INTRODUCTION

Pope Francis (born 1936) is indeed a great thinker because his writings push us beyond the comfortable little places that we build and curate to pursue our own interests. Those comfortable places can be parochial in the bad sense of the term: narrow and self-absorbed. In contrast, in the best Catholic sense, the parish (from which we get the word "parochial") is always and essentially united to the universal Church present in countless other nations, regions, languages, and ethnicities. The phrase "Little England" captures the negative parochial sense (see Cambridge Dictionary under "little Englander"); we can substitute the names of other countries when we limit ourselves to the comforts of our own nationalities. In my own country, the United States, we have a Trumpian, neo-isolationist version of the same notion that belittles our large, big-hearted continental nation. We can also see that negative parochialism as an exaggerated longing for the little shire and its comforts in a fantasy world. Those who have read Tolkien (or seen the movies released at the cusp and beginning of Francis's papacy) can instead recall that the hero becomes a hero precisely by leaving the shire.

As a Christian, I view Francis's call to go beyond our little, comfortable worlds as powerful because it echoes the powerful call made by Jesus of Nazareth who challenged his own nation to see the despised, multiethnic Samaritans as true neighbors worth emulating. At the heart of Francis's call is the idea and experience of love which many, both theists and nontheists, have described as a going out of ourselves towards the other. That central role of love (most distinctively as *agape* in the Greek of the New Testament) is theologically unsurprising since Christianity defines God as love (*agape*) itself (see 1 John 4:8,16, in the New Testament).

This book focuses on one of Pope Francis's encyclicals: *Fratelli Tutti* ("All Brethren") issued in 2020 on fraternity and social friendship (an encyclical is an authoritative teaching document issued by a Pope; see the References list for the link to this particular encyclical). *Fratelli Tutti* strings together many quotations from Francis' own previous remarks and writings. The encyclical is thus an excellent summary of Francis' thought. The other notable encyclical of Francis is *Laudato Si'* which focuses on ecology; but *Fratelli Tutti* is a good introduction, in my view, to Francis because of its more general scope. Francis' thought focuses on compassion for the poor and the marginalized (he often refers to the peripheries).

In the early nineteen sixties, Catholics had Pope John XXIII (1881-1963) known as "the good Pope" because of his humility and demonstrable compassion (see https://www.bbc.com/news/world-europe-27154491). In Francis, we have another "good Pope" also due to his striking humility and displays of compassion. (The phrase is used with all due respect to other virtuous popes with different styles and personalities.) While John XXIII had a very short pontificate, Francis in 2023 marks ten years as Pope. We thus have more writings and remarks available from *this* good Pope. My book makes use of that good fortune.

From the lengthy encyclical *Fratelli Tutti*, I have chosen to concentrate on five themes:

Chapter 1 The "Throwaway World";
Chapter 2 Embracing the Stranger;
Chapter 3 Beyond Borders;
Chapter 4 The Politics of Social Friendship;
Chapter 5 Dialogue as Social Friendship.

At several points, I refer to current events in some of my observations; this book reflects the realities and threats of 2023, especially in my own country, the United States. I close with an epilogue that focuses on the role of religion in the areas of concern sketched by Francis. The entire encyclical is freely available from the Vatican: https://www.humandevelopment.va/en/fratelli-tutti/enciclica.html.

The Pope's themes often intertwine in each section of the encyclical. Thus, the full development of a particular theme is a product of the encyclical as a whole and not only the product of a particular section of the encyclical.

Oswald Sobrino, Ph.D.
Lent/*Cuaresma* 2023

CHAPTER 1 THE "THROWAWAY WORLD"

◆ ◆ ◆

The phrase is that of Pope Francis (FT, heading at section 18; FT refers to *Fratelli Tutti*). If we see today a resurgence of fanaticism—reminiscent of that fanaticism which arose in Europe in the nineteen twenties and thirties, we also predictably see the rise of a throwaway world. The fanatic seeks to throw away differing views, opinions, and values. Unfortunately, fanaticism, true to form, goes all the way and seeks to throw away the persons who voice or represent those differing views, opinions, and persons. Sometimes, as in twentieth century Europe, we see the scourge of irrational wars of conquest. The example now in the third decade of the twenty-first century is the Russian war of conquest against an independent Ukraine. A nation that seeks to affirm its own sovereignty, culture, language, identity, and its identification with the West must in the eyes of the fanatics in Russia (not all Russians) be obliterated, destroyed, and reeducated so that those views and values disappear. For the Putin loyalist, Ukraine is a throwaway nation and culture. *Fratelli Tutti* dating from 2020 does not address the Ukrainian tragedy that arose in 2022, but the Pope's observations are prophetic of the Ukrainian situation in 2022 and beyond. This prophetic dimension arises from the Pope's reminder that today we, when mired in fanaticism, create throwaway worlds, nations, regions, and individuals.

Who are the throwaway individuals? Francis names them: the

poor, the disabled, the unborn, the elderly (FT, 18; all numeral citations to FT are section numbers, not page numbers). In other words, those who do not appear beautiful, superior, or powerful because of poverty, disability, unattained prenatal development, or the ravages of aging or disease. There is even the continuing presence of forms of slavery: "Whether by coercion, or deception, or by physical or psychological duress, human persons created in the image and likeness of God are deprived of their freedom, sold and reduced to being the property of others" (FT, 24; I usually omit double quotation marks when the Pope quotes, as he often does, other documents and remarks; you can locate the original source by directly examining online the citations in FT, which is in large part a compendium of Francis' earlier remarks on various issues). Recall that, as in the past, wars of conquest involve instances of enslavement—notice the Russian obsession with kidnapping Ukrainian children.

The other response to throwaway individuals and nations is to build walls: "the temptation to build a culture of walls, to raise walls, walls in the heart, walls on the land, in order to prevent this encounter with other cultures, with other people" (FT, 27). Francis continues: "And those who raise walls will end up as slaves within the very walls they have built. They are left without horizons, for they lack this interchange with others" (FT, 27). As scholars of slavery have pointed out, there arises a dependent relationship between the slave master and the enslaved—so that the slave masters are themselves shackled (compare Patterson, Ch. 12 "Slavery as Human Parasitism"). The example of Russia and Ukraine is also relevant here, but we can also add the relationship between the United States and Mexico.

By raising walls, individuals and nations lose the enrichment and new horizons of encountering the other who is different. Even an economist can see the absurd waste involved when nations—rather than deepening peaceful trading and cultural relations—choose to expend enormous resources on either conquest or on sealing off the other nation. In sum, "[i]solation and withdrawal into one's own interests are never the way to restore hope and bring about renewal" (FT, 30). Those claiming to make a nation "great again" by raising walls are engaged in deception, as we have seen in the United States under Trump and his imitators and in Hungary under Orbán. The deception in both nations has been centered on the fear of migrants, as noted by Francis without naming names: "Certain populist political regimes, as well as certain liberal economic approaches, maintain that an influx of migrants is to be prevented at all costs" (FT, 37). This deception has also extended to the pandemic that began in 2020 with the irrational refusal of some to protect others by following well-established public health measures such as vaccination and masking and the demagogic demonizing of dedicated public servants such as Dr. Anthony Fauci in the United States. As Francis points out, the pandemic shows that "we can only be saved together" (FT, 32) through mutual cooperation resulting in mutual protection.

This raising of walls and demonizing of the other yield a terrible harvest of what Francis calls "shameless aggression" (FT, 44). An American cannot avoid seeing an implied reference to Trump and to his opportunistic imitators in the United States and abroad: "Things that until a few years ago could not be said by anyone without risking the loss of universal respect can now be said with impunity, and in the crudest of terms, even by some political figures" (FT, 45). This crudity is amplified with "unparalleled room for expansion through computers and mobile devices" (FT, 44). Certain media outlets profit from this aggressive and deceptive speech as documented in litigation in the United States against the right-wing Fox News network owned by Rupert Murdoch.

The Pope's emphasis on not raising walls is important because the "process of building fraternity, be it local or universal, can only be undertaken by spirits that are free and open to authentic encounters" (FT, 50). Those encounters require embracing the stranger.

CHAPTER 2 EMBRACING THE STRANGER

◆ ◆ ◆

The stranger is someone very different from the norms to which we are accustomed and in which we feel safe and secure. I cannot help but think of the very short novel *The Stranger* by Albert Camus (1913-1960) which raises the question of who the stranger is. In the novel, a Frenchman living in Algeria exhibits a strange distance from typical emotional ties. This same Frenchman then kills, allegedly in self-defense, an Algerian Arab whose name is never given. We have in the end two strangers: the emotionally crippled Frenchman and the Arab unknown to the novel's readers. The result is that the Frenchman is convicted of murder and sentenced to death. It is a troubling book (see Lohnes https://www.britannica.com/topic/The-Stranger-novel-by-Camus).

As you can see, Francis' plea to embrace the stranger in *Fratelli Tutti* is not easy to put into practice. We have a natural and healthy fear of danger, and a stranger often triggers our sense of danger. In contrast to Camus' novel, Francis addresses the strangers among us through the well-known and ancient parable of the Good Samaritan (Luke 10:25-37, in the New Testament). There are two strangers in the parable: 1.) the man lying on the roadside wounded by robbers is a stranger because he is apparently unknown to those passing by on the road and 2.) the Samaritan rescuer of this wounded man is himself a despised ethnic and religious stranger to Jesus' Jewish audience. My assumption is that the wounded man on the roadside was Jewish like Jesus' audience. The foreign Samaritan not only tends to the wounds of the Jewish man but also pays for him to stay at an inn to recuperate and guarantees to the innkeeper the payment of any additional expenses. He makes reparations for a crime that he did not commit.

In contrast to this generous foreign rescuer who "came near" to the wounded man, two Jewish religious officials who had previously seen this wounded fellow Jew "passed by on the other side" (see the version of Luke 10:25-37, at FT 56). Jesus dramatically asks his audience which of these three travelers "was a neighbor to the man who fell into the hands of the robbers" (Id.). The Jewish lawyer whose initial questioning of Jesus had sparked the parable answered without hesitation: "The one who showed him mercy" (Id.). The drama of the parable emerges strongly in the cultural context of that time and place:

> The parable, though, is troubling, for Jesus says that the wounded man was a Judean, while the one who stopped and helped him was a Samaritan. This detail is quite significant for our reflection on a love that includes everyone. The Samaritans lived in a region where pagan rites were practiced. For the Jews, this made them impure, detestable, dangerous (FT, 82).

Here Jesus is criticizing the religious prejudices of his fellow believers. Supposed piety can itself become an excuse for impious behavior toward the other.

As in Camus, the stranger is a threat—the wounded and unknown human being is a threat as an interruption to my daily duties and activities and a potential threat to my budget. As others have surely pointed out over the centuries, the wounded man in the parable might have been part of a ruse by the robbers to trap others who would stop and look, just as American motorists today are prudently careful when they see an apparently disabled car on the side of the highway or a hitchhiker near a prison. The stranger is also a threat in the person of the good foreigner who aids the wounded man in the parable—foreign in ethnicity and in religious practices. The very goodness of the despised foreigner is a threat because his actions subvert the stereotypes with which we are comfortable and by implication condemn our own detachment from the wounded among our own.

Thus, the stranger can come in many forms. He can be the person native to our own land who urgently needs our help as a matter of life or death, or he can be the foreigner whose presence we hate. Jesus masterfully brings these two challenging strangers together in one narrative and anticipates the two strangers (French and Arab) in Camus' own narrative. For it is clear, at least to me, that the emotionally strange Frenchman described by Camus was emotionally wounded and himself in need of some kind of rescue. And, of course, the Arab stranger needed proactive protection by the authorities rather than merely post-mortem judicial procedures.

From the ancient parable of Jesus, Francis draws forth several practical conclusions. The first is that the call to mercy is "universal in scope, embracing everyone on the basis of our shared humanity" (FT, 60). The second is that the parable is a call to avoid forming "closed and isolated groups" (FT, 62). The latter point is a constant and recurring theme in the thought of Pope Francis. Again and again he emphasizes that, both within the Church and outside the Church, individuals must avoid sealing themselves off within closed groups. A Church parish cannot be just a gathering of longstanding cliques as if a parish were an exclusive cult or movement within an otherwise universal Church. Likewise in our daily secular lives our involvement cannot just be limited to exclusive associations and clubs some of which, historically, have excluded different ethnicities, races, classes, and religions. I recall here my own memories of living in my ostensibly Catholic native city of New Orleans which was notoriously ridden with socially prominent organizations excluding for decades and still today those from different ethnic, racial, and social class backgrounds as if it were normal and unquestionable. Even in politics we should strive for spaces in which different points of view (excluding those advocating racism, sexism, unjust discrimination, or violence) can be freely and respectfully exchanged. Our social lives should not be limited to exclusive alumni or professional associations. Democratic civic life requires social spaces in which we encounter the friendship of those different from us in appearance, in life experiences, and in beliefs. That is the concrete testimony required for those who claim to believe that we as humans have a common Creator of one human family. At the same time, by avoiding the exclusion of those different from us, we ourselves are rewarded with unlimited personal enrichment on many levels.

Francis also does not hesitate to call for a radical change in attitude toward the weak: "Let us admit that, for all the progress we have made, we are still 'illiterate' when it comes to accompanying, caring for and supporting the most frail and vulnerable members of our developed societies. We have become accustomed to looking the other way, passing by, or ignoring situations until they affect us directly" (FT, 64). Many in our American cities (and in cities overseas) live in neighborhoods full of crime, fear, and violence (plus dirty and unhealthy conditions). No one should be left to the mercy of criminal activity. No one, such as the elderly, should be locked into homes because they are easy targets for criminals preying on the weak. No city is worthy of its name and all its glitzy public relations if that city looks the other way in these situations. Moreover, it is often the poorest who suffer the worst effects of environmental pollution whether they are people in Flint, Michigan, or in other cities, whose drinking water has been poisoned, or people in rural areas such as East Palestine, Ohio, whose homes have become uninhabitable and whose bodies have been poisoned because a wealthy railroad corporation neglected to pursue the safest way to do business.

Yet there is good news that we also observe daily. We see the father gently and joyfully carrying his disabled daughter to school every morning. We see parents seeking a richer life for their children whose abilities are limited. It is not an accident that readers of the Gospels often see parents assertively and dramatically seeking out Jesus to heal their children (see, for example, the moving episodes in Mark 5:21-43; 7:24-30; and 9:14-29). We see older sons and daughters caring for their parents despite other pressing demands. For, yes, even those biologically related to us who are weak and disabled can become strangers whom we relegate to institutions and whom we wish to ignore. Beyond the family circle, we see teachers and students bringing education and culture to those who are imprisoned. Many religious and non-religious organizations encourage their members to undertake service trips to deprived areas of their own country or even beyond their borders. In sum, we see the great alternative to the narcissistic, egotistical lifestyle: "anyone who is neither a robber nor a passer-by is either injured himself or **bearing an injured person on his shoulders**" (FT, 70; emphasis added). The Pope's words remind us of Vergil's unforgettable image of Aeneas bearing his elderly father Anchises on his shoulders as their city collapsed. We see that daily heroism everywhere; but the current situation in Ukraine is a powerful instance, although there are still voices shamefully calling for the West to look the other way.

Notably the Pope does not spare the religious from this challenging critique:

> I sometimes wonder why, in the light of this [call to embrace the stranger], it took so long for the Church unequivocally to condemn slavery and various forms of violence. Today, with our developed spirituality and theology, we have no excuses. Still, there are those who appear to feel encouraged or at least permitted by

their faith to support varieties of narrow and violent nationalism, xenophobia and contempt, and even the mistreatment of those who are different (FT, 86).

We see this religious barbarity when the Orthodox Patriarch of Moscow supports the Russian state's invasion and destruction of Ukraine. We also see this religious barbarity when conservative Christians in the United States applaud politicians who separate children from parents at our southern border or unjustly discriminate against those from other religious backgrounds. We have the scandal of misguided Christians eagerly embracing political antichrists with shocking ease—political antichrists adept at manipulating religious sentiments by waiving Bibles or scapegoating those who are different. Embracing the stranger means going beyond the borders or divisions that appear within the same country and between countries, as the next chapter explains.

CHAPTER 3 BEYOND BORDERS

◆ ◆ ◆

Love "capable of transcending borders is the basis of what in every city and country can be called 'social friendship'. Genuine social friendship within a society makes true universal openness possible" (FT, 99). In Chapter 4, we will consider the politics of social friendship in detail. But, for now, social friendship signals the apex of the Pope's encyclical. In embracing social friendship, the Pope imagines a world that more and more goes beyond viewing individuals as mere " 'associates' " who play only the role of "partners in the pursuit of particular interests" (FT, 102). That is why the issues raised by Pope Francis go beyond our job titles, our citizenship, and other sociological categories. Francis is speaking of our fundamental stance toward others, a stance that is deeper than our outward sociological slots. In religious terms, Francis is speaking of our chosen spirituality —a spirituality which either we choose or which society and custom will impose on us. That spirituality is how we approach life: are others mere partners for advancing allied interests, or are they friends whose own true good we take seriously? Christian spirituality is rooted in the recognition that the Creator of all human beings is love itself and thus points to the love of social friendship as the most profound and fulfilling way of relating to others.

One major "border" that we often see is that between those deemed valuable and those deemed lacking in value. Francis points especially to the situation of the economically powerless and the disabled:

> Every human being has the right to live with dignity and to develop integrally [wholly or completely]; this fundamental right cannot be denied by any country. People have this right even if they are unproductive, or were born with or developed limitations. This does not detract from their great dignity as human persons, a dignity based not on circumstances but on the intrinsic worth of their being. Unless this basic principle is upheld, there will be no future either for fraternity or for the survival of humanity (FT, 107).

The disdain toward the unproductive or disabled creates internal borders within the same community and builds walls between countries. When social friendship replaces such disdain, the open world beyond borders that Francis celebrates becomes an increasing reality in daily life.

This commitment to the full development of each individual requires recognizing that the right to private property is never absolute but is always conditioned on promoting the good of all—a notion which is a fundamental Catholic teaching (see FT, 120). That Catholic teaching is known as "the universal destination of created goods" (FT, 120). How many political conservatives take that Catholic teaching seriously? How many politically conservative Catholics take that teaching seriously? Is it merely an easily ignored, irrelevant aspiration? Or is it a realistic teaching for political implementation? With so many Catholics holding high positions in all branches of the U.S. government, one would think that the universal destination of created goods would be foremost in their minds. That is certainly not the case. The universal destination of all created goods means that we cannot tolerate internal or external borders that relegate others to poverty and despair, while we have more than our share of created goods.

In a great understatement, Francis notes that "[c]ertainly, all this calls for an alternative way of thinking" (FT, 127). That revolutionary way of thinking means the conviction that "if all people are my brothers and sisters, and if the world truly belongs to everyone, then it matters little whether my neighbor was born in my country or elsewhere" (FT, 125). Many right-wing politicians—even those who strongly claim a religious identity—think the opposite, namely, that only those in my group or those of sufficient ethnic purity are brothers and sisters and that economic wealth belongs only to those with legal title to it. In other words, the world belongs to the most powerful regardless of how they acquired that power. In place of the Judeo-Christian ethic that requires sharing with the poor (an ethic also present in some other traditions), such right-wing politicians canonize selfishness. That is why right-wing ideology is ultimate sterile; it is simply a naked assertion of power with no moral dimension, usually dressed up with atavistic appeals to race, nationalism, and contempt for those who are different or weak. Prophetic leaders in all areas should propose and incarnate a very different way of thinking to ensure peace and progress for all.

But the pull toward atavistic savagery as a way of viewing the other persists. After so many catastrophic twentieth-century dictators, Russian and China, and many minor nations, are still in the grips of dictators. Even in the United States, there is the eeriness of a governor in Florida proposing previously unimaginable restrictions on academic freedom and on free political speech; and a compliant Florida state legislature is eager to please its "great" leader. The strongman still appeals to the emotionally weak looking for someone to follow who promises all the answers. We must go beyond borders, but there is a strong pull everywhere to fortify borders and division, even by some within the Catholic Church served by Pope Francis. As a remedy, the next chapter discusses the politics required by social friendship.

CHAPTER 4 THE POLITICS OF SOCIAL FRIENDSHIP

◆ ◆ ◆

As we have seen, for Pope Francis, social friendship embraces the common God-given human dignity of each person regardless of ability, age, ethnicity, race, economic income, or country of birth. Like so much in our world, the fate of social friendship significantly depends on the kind of politics that we have. Here is a true exercise in *Realpolitik* by the Pope who recognizes that mere rhetoric about fraternity and social friendship is not enough. In the Christian tradition, the New Testament makes clear that nice, pious talk is not sufficient to meet our moral obligations to each other:

> [14] What good is it, my brothers and sisters, if someone claims to have faith but does not have works? Surely that faith cannot save, can it? [15] If a brother or sister is naked and lacks daily food [16] and one of you says to them, "Go in peace; keep warm and eat your fill," and yet you do not supply their bodily needs, what is the good of that? [17] So faith by itself, if it has no works, is dead (James 2:14-17, NRSV Updated Edition).

Thus, social friendship—that, by definition, goes beyond personal friendships—requires a new type of politics.

The Pope refers to the opposite of a politics of social friendship: the politics of "unhealthy 'populism' " (FT, 159). In the United

States, we see this unhealthy populism which exploits and exacerbates division in Trump and in his progeny like DeSantis and others. In Europe, we see Putin in Russia and Orbán in Hungary. In my view, these politicians "seek popularity by appealing to the basest and most selfish inclinations of certain sectors of the population. This becomes all the more serious when, whether in cruder or more subtle forms, it leads to the usurpation of institutions and laws" (FT, 159). History and current events show that the main targets of such unhealthy populism are freedom of speech, freedom of the press, and academic freedom. Encroachments on these freedoms signal dictatorship even under ostensibly democratic forms. As is his practice, the Pope does not name individuals or countries. But, in my view, the implicated individuals and countries are not difficult to identify.

The Pope diagnoses the defect at the core of this type of politics in which "the proclivity to selfishness" predominates so that the only concerns are "with myself, my group, my petty interests" (FT, 166; the Pope uses the traditional Christian term for such inclinations to selfishness: "concupiscence"). On the international level, the continued vigor of the United Nations is, in the Pope's view, essential to elevate international relations beyond destructive and unjust acts (see FT, 172-73).

The political vision of the Pope radically opposes the vision of those dividing citizens by income, race, ethnicity, religion, culture, and abilities. For the Pope and the Catholic Church, the social and political realms must be expressions of charity or neighborly love as seen in the parable of the Good Samaritan that we have examined : "charity finds expression not only in close and intimate relationships but also in 'macroeconomic relationships: social, economic and political' " (FT, 181). Charity as a theological and ethical vision for society does not prescind from the truths produced by the physical and social sciences because it "respects the development of the sciences and their essential contribution to finding the surest and most practical means of achieving the desired results. For when the good of others is at stake, good intentions are not enough. Concrete efforts must be made to bring about whatever they and their nations need for the sake of their development" (FT, 185). This high respect for the fruits of human scientific discoveries is consistent with the best in Catholicism's ancient commitment to education. The Pope's affirmation that we must find the practical means to yield concrete progress is, in my view, similar to insights found in the philosophical school of American Pragmatism (see my book *5 Lessons from John Dewey*; compare FT, 212-14).

What kind of politics seeks the common good (see FT, 180) of all? The Pope outlines this program for the common good:

> [L]et us be committed to living and teaching the value of respect for others, a love capable of welcoming differences, and the priority of the dignity of every human being over his or her ideas, opinions, practices, and even sins. Even as forms of fanaticism, closedmindedness and social and cultural fragmentation proliferate in present-day society, a good politician will take the first step and insist that different voices be heard. . . . [U]niformity proves stifling and leads to cultural decay (FT, 191).

In contrast, the destructive demagogue, becoming more common even in the democratic West, is an agent of division and suppression of human freedom using the "sharp and aggressive tone" of social media and offering a "monologue" rather than seeking the encounter of dialogue (see FT, 200). Small minds and hearts offer only a monologue. True leaders who think big and seek room for all advance culture instead of creating cultural decay that also results in economic decay. A politics based on social friendship and honest consensus avoids the atrophy of culture and civilization and creates the conditions for the progress that all desire (see FT, 179). Throughout history, we see that open societies with freedom of speech and debate advance the quality of life; while closed, authoritarian societies, whether based on imposed political or religious uniformity, fail to improve the cultural and economic conditions of life.

CHAPTER 5 DIALOGUE AS SOCIAL FRIENDSHIP

◆ ◆ ◆

The politics of social friendship is a politics of encounter, and the means of encounter is dialogue. In plain English, we can say that dialogue is "talking things through." The Greek etymology of "dialogue" bears this out since "*dia*" means "through" (see https://www.merriam-webster.com/dictionary/dialogue). Plato's dialogues at the beginning of Western civilization set an example of developing consensus through question and answer. So what the Pope proposes is, of course, not new at all. In the Christian tradition, we have the parables of Jesus which aim to shock an audience into viewing things from a very different perspective, as we have seen in the parable of the Good Samaritan arising from the dialogue between Jesus and a Jewish lawyer. As in Plato, the goal is to reorient the thinking and the possibilities imagined by those engaged in dialogue.

Dialogue is hard, especially when the other is very different and when the topics are very controversial. Francis is calling us as individuals and as nations to attempt something very difficult; but it can be done because, throughout history, treaties, constitutions, and legislation do emerge from negotiations and dialogue. The first step is a new way of living: "To speak of a 'culture of encounter' means that we, as a people, should be passionate about meeting others, seeking points of contact, building bridges, planning a project that includes everyone. This becomes an aspiration and a style of life" (FT, 216). Fundamental to this new personal style is letting go of the mania for uniformity that is a great weakness in too many insecure human personalities, whether in private or in public matters.

Francis provides this extended comment on the necessity of embracing those who are different:

> All this calls for the ability to recognize other people's right to be themselves and to be different. This recognition, as it becomes a culture, makes possible the creation of a social covenant. Without it, subtle ways can be found to make others insignificant, irrelevant, of no value to society. While rejecting certain visible forms of violence, another more insidious kind of violence can take root: the violence of those who despise people who are different, especially when their demands in any way compromise their own particular interests (FT, 218).

We see the inability to embrace people who are different in the controversies currently taking place in the United States. One right-wing Republican governor (DeSantis in Florida) is advancing his ambitions for higher office by targeting the teaching of the history of black slavery in schools. Black slavery, as others have said, is the original sin of American society which enmeshed not only the South but also the North. The origins and early history of many prestigious American institutions (and the biographies of many famous historical American figures) are intertwined with the economic profits made from the horrific practice of black slavery. The right-wing governor in Florida wants to squelch a profound, historical recognition of that original sin. He also targets other groups who are different in their lifestyles and identities. This drive for imposed uniformity will surely fail, but there will be much unnecessary distress and conflict for the duration with a high opportunity cost.

Instead of focusing on constructive dialogue to develop consensus on practical issues, demagogic politicians deemphasize pressing issues such as the lack of access to health care, the high cost of medication, and the need for a higher minimum wage without absurd delays and instead emphasize creating new enemies. Pope Francis notes that in some situations we see "a tendency to deliberately fabricate enemies" (FT, 266).

The roots of this fear of the other who is different lie in the psychology of the human personality. The demagogues accentuate that fear to achieve grandiose personal ambitions for power. Society suffers and pays the high cost to subsidize the unhealthy drive of such grandiose ambitions. Society does not move forward and so decays. In contrast, Pope Francis proposes a different path and outlines what is required to advance on the "paths of renewed encounter" (heading at FT, 225). The first requirement is quite striking because we often assume that it has no place in the hard world of politics: "we can choose to cultivate kindness" (FT, 222). This kindness frees us from amnesia concerning the needs and rights of others (see FT, 223-24). This type of kindness is the opposite of the macho, in-your-face political style of the typical demagogue. The public must reject any taste for that brutal style of politics. The best guarantee of law and order in society is to reject amnesia concerning the economically desperate, whether at home or abroad: "When a society – whether local, national or global – is willing to leave a part of itself on the fringes, no political programmes or resources spent on law enforcement or surveillance systems can indefinitely guarantee tranquility" (FT, 235).

Pope Francis also calls for something even more difficult than dialogue: forgiveness. What he means by forgiveness is giving up anger and the quest for "taking revenge and destroying the other" (FT, 242). Yet forgiveness does not mean abandoning self-defense:

> Nor does this mean calling for forgiveness when it involves renouncing our own rights, confronting corrupt officials, criminals or those who would debase our dignity. We are called to love everyone, without exception; at the same time, loving an oppressor does not mean allowing him to keep oppressing us, or letting him think that what he does is acceptable. . . . Forgiveness does not entail allowing oppressors to keep trampling on their own dignity and that of others, or letting criminals continue their wrongdoing. Those who suffer injustice have to defend strenuously their own rights and those of their family, precisely because they must preserve the dignity they have received as a loving gift from God. If a criminal has harmed me or a loved one, no one can forbid me from demanding justice and ensuring that this person – or anyone else – will not harm me, or others, again. This is entirely just; forgiveness does not forbid it but actually demands it (FT, 241).

I have extensively quoted the Pope's description of self-defense because, unfortunately, often preachers (with good intentions) describe forgiveness in a partial and haphazard way as if forgiveness requires the abandonment of self-defense. When people hear such a partial and nonsensical description of forgiveness, they shrug their shoulders and simply dismiss the preacher as living in a fantasy world. As Francis notes, forgiveness insists on legitimate self-defense at all times for the sake of the common good of everyone involved in a particular situation.

In remarks that are apt for those grappling with the legacy of slavery in the United States, the Pope makes clear that "[f]orgiving does not mean forgetting" (FT, 250):

> We can never move forward without remembering

the past; we do not progress without an honest and unclouded memory. We need to "keep alive the flame of collective conscience, bearing witness to succeeding generations to the horror of what happened", because that witness "awakens and preserves the memory of the victims, so that the conscience of humanity may rise up in the face of every desire for dominance and destruction" (FT, 249).

Thus, the demagogic quest to eliminate full and honest confrontation with the original sin of slavery in the United States is a path to failure, division, and even disorder. The convenient emotional amnesia of those who profited from past oppression is irrational, not only morally but also politically and socially.

Francis points to "two extreme situations" that require a new focus on forgiveness: war and the death penalty (FT, 255). He warns against "an overly broad interpretation" of the Church's traditional criteria for a just war, given the massive power for destruction that nations now possess (FT, 258). As I understand Francis, he is calling for viewing the option of war as highly suspect. We presume that war is the least desirable option for any nation to undertake because of its uncontrollable, destructive consequences. Unfortunately, the irrational still controls large and powerful nations, such as Putin's Russia, which choose war even if it is self-destructive. Dialogue should replace the option of war.

As to the death penalty, the Pope restates the current teaching of the Catholic Church "that 'the death penalty is inadmissible' and [that] the Church is firmly committed to calling for its abolition worldwide" (FT, 263). But again society has the right of self-defense which can be vindicated by means excluding the death penalty (FT, 267). In my view, that right of self-defense requires a responsible, realistic, and highly prudent system of courts, magistrates, and judges who keep the truly dangerous away from the rest of society so that an outraged society no longer feels the need to clamor for the death penalty. Such legitimate self-defense requires, in my view, a robust dialogue among all involved in the criminal justice system to effectively protect society from violence of any kind.

EPILOGUE: THE ROLE OF RELIGION

◆ ◆ ◆

What role can religion play in promoting social friendship and its call for a new politics based on a dialogue of encounter with those who are different? Pope Francis' analysis based on the spiritual values of human dignity for all and of charity or selfless love has already answered that question. But, at the end of the encyclical, the Pope provides more detail on the role of religion in fostering a new way of relating to those who are different. For the Pope, religions that proclaim "respect for each human person as a creature called to be a child of God" provide the objective and transcendent basis for respecting the other despite differences and for encountering the other in love (FT, 271). More bluntly, "without an openness to the Father of all, there will be no solid and stable reasons for an appeal to fraternity" (FT, 272; see also FT, 273). The Fatherhood of God the Creator is the birthright of each human being regardless of religious tradition or lack thereof. There is clearly no limiting identity as children of God only to those belonging to a particular tradition. The Creator as Father is a universal gift for all human beings.

The distinctive Christian view bases our identity as children of God *in its most profound, intimate, and fullest form* in the sonship of Jesus Christ through whom Christians become adopted children of God (see FT, 277 and, in the New Testament, Romans 8:14-16). Yet Christians seek dialogue and encounter with other religions

ABOUT THE AUTHOR

Oswald Sobrino

Oswald Sobrino holds a Ph.D. in Latin and Roman Studies (University of Florida). He has taught at the college level for many years.

www.ingramcontent.com/pod-product-compliance
Lightning Source LLC
Chambersburg PA
CBHW050710250726
48662CB00002B/939

and tolerance of all religions because "as children of the one God, we are all brothers and sisters" (FT, 279). The love of God as Father includes even atheists (FT, 281). Thus, religious differences must never add to the many causes of violence and hatred already present in the world. Large numbers of Christians also invoke the motherhood of Mary who intercedes in prayer for all humanity (FT, 278).

Before ending, it is good to return to the parable of the Good Samaritan. We are called to care for the wounds of all—whether they share our religion, ethnicity, social class, or beliefs. All are children of God, and thereby all are part of one great human brotherhood and sisterhood. All indeed are brethren, *fratelli tutti*. That conviction is a major pillar in the legacy of Pope Francis.